Crowe Press LLC
www.crowepress.com
ISBN: 978-1-939484-09-3
Copyright Marta Moran Bishop 2013
www.martamoranbishop.com

A POET'S JOURNEY

SUNLIGHT AND SHADOWS

MARTA MORAN BISHOP

Index

TABLE OF CONTENTS

Index

This book is dedicated to my husband, who is the backbone of my existence. He is always there for me emotionally, he is the most supportive person I have ever known, a person cannot ask for more.

A POET'S JOURNEY

SUNLIGHT AND SHADOWS

MARTA MORAN BISHOP

ABUSED

I lie upon the floor
Blood dripping from your latest blows
Curled in a ball, crying silently
Heart and soul trampled once more

Black hole inside of me
Lost, confused, and alone
Can't walk, stand nor move
Except for retching, sobbing

Wish for nothingness now
So I hear not your words
Those hate filled screams of yours

You're no good without me
Stupid, loser, woman
Flighty, flaky, brainless
I heard so many times

Way too many to count
The times you left me there
Spirit broken in two
Shattered, beaten, bloodied.

SHACKLED

Shackled inside myself
Isolated, alone
I've done it to myself
Afraid I'll lose again
All those who comfort me

Can I learn a new way
At this late stage of life
To not feel so alone
Careless about others
And their thoughts about me

Will the time ever come
When I'm free to be me
While in that crowded room
Unafraid of outcome
Feeling wanted again

Not a stranger alone
Afraid to share secrets
Mostly that I am shy
And cringe when you are near
Fearing you'll think me odd.

FALLING APART

I'm hanging on by a thread
This round of work without play
Constant demands on my time
Lacking sleep, working nonstop

It's sure to pull me in two
Need to stop, laugh a little
Dance, sing, and throw my arms wide
Smell the roses, hug a cat

Pull my pieces together
Ride like the wind, scream aloud
Follow my dreams once again
Before I am pulled apart.

MELANCHOLY

I am melancholy today
The past memories creeping in
Of times and days with my loved ones
Who had left, long ago past on

Into another life they've gone
Where I can't touch, see, or hear them
A sadness washes through me now
With the knowledge of my loss

Hopes and prayers for strong winds to come
To blow through the tangled thoughts
Stir the pot full of memories
Pull out those bright and cheerful ones

For when that final curtain descends
And I have passed from this life
I'll see again all those I've loved
On the rainbow bridge we'll meet

My heart filled with light and gladness
All hurts and troubles behind me
Promise of a new life ahead
If I let go of the painful days
And take only the love with me.

SIXTY-NINE DAYS

Sixty-nine days she lay dying
Sixty-nine without food
Sixty-nine days we all waited

At her bedside or across the world
Sixty-nine days with broken hearts
Sixty-nine days and more of crying.

CARETAKER

When the stress got too much
And the burden too great
A dream I created
To help me through life

The black hole was too deep
To my soul it did go
For myself I had lost
Clinging tightly to life

Not a soul understood
None tried very hard
My reasons were lame
My mind in a mess

Many called me crazy
I suppose they were right
I was very busy
Clinging tightly to life

Illusions and visions
Brought me some light
To break the depression
To cease the hard fight.

Sunlight and Shadows

Like a phoenix I rise
Out of ashes and dust
Life returns to these limbs
My heart is made whole

I pick up the pieces
Relearn who I am
Pull strings back together
Of whom I once was

I will miss you forever
Our lives so entwined
Together so long
Now endlessly apart

Knowing you made me better
Though at the time I was less
Now our conflict is gone
My burden put down

A hug would have helped
A shoulder to weep on
A thought for the plight
When my strength was long gone.

Marta Moran Bishop

Instead the world left me
To handle it alone
The trips to hospital
And the fear for your life

To watch you decline
Alone and bereft
Like a phoenix I rise
With the gift you gave me.

PANIC

Breathe, breathe, breath I tell myself
As the panic attacks rip through me

Why now, are they coming, I ask
But no response is forthcoming

Shadowy closet beacons me
Curl up and hide in my dark womb.

WHAT ONCE WAS

Once upon a time
I thought there was love
Betrayal was yours
The trust is long gone

A family we were
At least so I thought
Pretending no hurt
Even through neglect

Let go of the lies
You told about me
To make me look bad
So you could look good

I wish it was different
My eyes opened now
Reality clear
A doormat I'm not

I cannot go back
To playing your role
A fantasy game
Where you care for me.

Extension of you
When needed I am
A mirror for you
To see your beauty in

Goodbye to you all
Who once were family
My heart will still bleed
From the loss of love

Though it was a dream
Not reality
Still sadness will cling
To memories past.

INVISIBLE

Have you ever felt invisible
Alone in a room full of people
Standing there, no clue what to say

Just a round penny in a square hole
Wondering if you will ever fit
Or continue being the outcast.

LIFE'S JOURNEY

Life's journey is short
From daylight to dusk
We long for the return
To the closeness we lost

The dawn of our lives
To each of us comes
The day we are thrust
Into this world
And take our first step
Toward separation.

Marta Moran Bishop

INNOCENCE LOST

You were only fourteen
When innocence was lost
And he was thirty-five
A sister's husband too
A man for you to trust

Instead he was frightening
Slyly ogling you
Your nipples so ripe
Young and virginal girl
It's not my fault he said

When stealing innocence
You tempted me you see
With young virginity
And nipples oh so ripe
Budding and blossoming

Shame lay deeply in you
Now hide your head young girl
For it must be your fault
After all he told you so
And he was the adult.

A WOMAN'S HEART

I'm a woman who'll give
Till my heart has hardened
My spirit is broken
Abuse my trust I'm gone
I won't willingly stay.

Wrap your arms around me
Cocoon me near your heart
Keep my essence embraced
Let your fingers caress
And your lips touch my soul

Honor me, my purpose
You don't have to agree
Difference is healthy
Respect my position
And I'll give you my heart

With distrust you'll lose me
Lies will disillusion
Jealousy will harm us
Lack of kind words destroy
The love for each other.

BRIGHT SPIRIT SHOW US THE WAY

Friendship based on shadows
Promises never kept
Lines crossed too often
With words misunderstood

Can we survive this way
When we cannot be honest
Platitudes often spoken
Without substance or truth

Honor, kindness is lost
So, mired in pretense
Arise my true sister
Throw off your raiments of fear
Take my hand in yours

Let light bind us together
Our words build each other
No tears to squash our dreams
No anger to close our hearts.

Arm in arm together
Women can change the world
Grow, let go of our past
Fearless, strong and loving
Bright spirit show the way.

Marta Moran Bishop

LOST ONES

A tear runs down my face
Eyes brimming with sadness
The loss of little ones
Whose wings will not open
Nor learn to fly on air

Brighten the world with joy
A life lost, world shattered
For lack of civility
Loss much too heartbreaking
Lacking care for another

To produce only fighting
Why we ask of each other
Emptiness is answered
Guns in schools, guards in homes
Will we learn our lessons?

HATE

Hate filled words race across the page
They speak of angry destruction
Little children screaming loudly
It must be my way or no way

They speak ill of minorities
And all those who don't think their way
Misery, animosity they spread
Around the world, onto their children

What makes them chose to hate others
Wishing others to bow to them
Recognizing them as supreme
Why are they so fearful of change?

It must be fear that is inside them
Making them hate so much
I see nothing else to cause this
Fear of the unknown is the source.

CIVILITY

What is the difference you say
Between help and lecturing
It's because I love you, is said
As you verbally abuse me

I want you to be the very best
You write with words that beat me down
Everyone will think you horrid
If you do not do it my way

No one does this you say again
About things you disagree with
No one likes people who do that
You say, speaking for everyone

I will respect your boundaries
I won't accept the lecturing
What could be said in one sentence
Is stated in a million words

The difference between the two
Is the tone, the length and the words
All civility is lacking
No respect is in your speech
Honesty is good and helps
But not without courtesy.

I'M A WOMAN

I'm a living, breathing person
I think, work, and love as you do
I'm not an extension of you
Nor am I a part of the house
Not just mother or grandmother

I'm not a breeding animal
Nor a child needing a parent
I'm a woman with desires
The need to be loved, heard, and seen
Recognized as a human being.

YOU SHOULD HAVE KNOWN

Some will say we are past our prime
Experience is thrown away
Today, the young are all that count
Old man, old woman your time has passed

Not our issue if you can't survive
You should have saved, you should have known
Too bad, it was wasted on those kids.
So what if your job is no more.

So what the company has moved
Your skills are no longer needed
Old man, old woman your time has passed
You should have known, you should have saved.

You say I am only forty
Or maybe fifty or sixty
With many good years in front of me
What does that matter now?

The young need it more than you do
They come cheap that's all that matters
We don't care if you have no way
To feed or clothe yourself.

Experience means nothing now
The younger, the better they say
Their future is in front of them
Old man, old woman your time has passed.

You should have saved, you should have known
That you too would be older soon
You are just a consumer now
Not a person, not important

Alas, the world has lost its light
Instead knowledge is thrown away
Putting all hope on ignorance
Holding onto the belief
People are interchangeable.

UNDERSTANDING

You say I'm nuts, you say you know
I don't do things the way you do
My laughter isn't quite like yours
I don't dress the same way either

How can you judge what you don't know
Who gave you the right to decide
What is right or wrong for me
When you don't know what makes me tick

You haven't lived life in my shoes
Nor have you seen my heart and loves
No effort to understand
What makes me tick, what makes me laugh.

A WRITER'S DREAMS

Writing is a passion
I couldn't live without

Haunted by the story
That turns inside my head

The thought, emotion, line
Begging to be released

Will not stop till it's told
Ever running circles
Around inside my mind.

PETER

Before I saw your face or touched your fur
I heard your cries for help, longing for love
So loud your anguish I knew where to go
So deep your despair you didn't know me

For a home of your own, all hope was gone
Tossed out by family to fend for yourself
Frightened, alone on the streets you were found
Age guessed at, circumstances unknown

Just a big friendly orange cat, sadly un-kept
They said you were two or three, maybe four
Fifteen short years we have been together
If I am lucky we'll have a few more

Age is showing, spring gone from your step
Still there are moments when you jump and play
At night, asleep your paw clings to my hand
Your eyes filled with love when you gaze at me

We lost our Sheba and Billy's gone too
Smudge and Poofie passed through that final door
Momma Pat is long gone and waits for you
I've begged, pleaded for a little more time.

Now you warn me your time is coming
I am not ready I never will be
If I'm lucky we'll have many more years
Before you pass, beyond the life we have shared

Little Peter, you've taught me so much
The depth of the joy you daily give me
Will long be with me and not forgotten
Until that time comes our lives are as one.

THE DANCE

We'll dance amongst the stars tonight.
Weave webs of shimmering light
Across the clouds our feet will fly
Tripping the light fantastic

Singing our songs of hope and love
Our voices filling the air
Silver notes of glistening sound
Making waves of light and joy.

From star to star we'll weave our web
Gleaming strands of golden net
Leaving behind a trail of light
For those who'll join our dance.

SHADOWS

Shadows play across the walls
From dawn to dusk follow me
Even on cloudy, windswept days
They are waiting for me and thee

Alas, the day your shadow goes
And no longer follows me
For on that day the sun has gone
Your smile has left my life

Darkness falls and sunlight vanishes
Gone the days our shadows entwine
No longer walking side by side
And mine stands alone once more.

Marta Moran Bishop

LOVE NEVER DIES

In sunlight or moonlight
Dancing rainbows of color
Decorate each strand of hair
As it cascades down her back

Star kissed eyes twinkle with love
As his hands gently caress
Arms intertwined together
Stealing a kiss in twilight

Long will the memories last
In heart and mind as he stands
Looking at the lonely stone
Where her name is deeply etched.

LOST LOVE

The breeze moves through the trees
Whispering where are you
Friend of my heart what happened
Long ago you left me

Lost, alone without you
Never to hear your voice
Nor see your face again
All sparkle is gone now

Life's bereft without you
Cold winds across my soul
Upon my heart ice clings
No warmth, no fire left.

Marta Moran Bishop

KINDNESS

Kindness is in your eyes
The touch of your hands
Sweet breath of life given
Heartfelt hope is shown

A smile and a laugh
Shared merriment too
Nice are the words you speak
Gentle is your touch

Encompassing soul
The fire in your eyes
Is joy brought and given
To all whom you meet.

SUNLIGHT AND SHADOWS

Darkness and despair
Will follow you through life
When allowed to hold sway
If you don't look for the light

Loss and confusion
Will mark all your days
When shadows explain you
And sunlight is not

Look for the sunbeam
In every cloud above
Follow every rainbow
To find the rays of light

Hold onto sunshine
Each beam and hint of light
Let starlight deep inside
And moonlight define you

Find that place inside
Where you can see the light
Nourish it forever
And shadows will take flight.

Marta Moran Bishop

I WONDER

I wonder if when I die
In the afterlife I'll recall
The name I carried all these years
Or will I leave it in my grave?

Will our names still matter then
Will we care what we once were called
It's just a part of our façade
In that great, lovely here-after

Is it how we lived our lives
And not our personalities
Nor our physical attributes
That stay with us beyond the grave

Instead our inner beauty shines
And brings us to a higher plane
A place our names are forgotten
Because, we are all born a new.

IF YOU BELIEVE

If you believe in God
Be it male or female
And you call on your God
Think you, he or she cares

If you call God Buddha
Jehovah or Krishna
Morgaine or Astarte
Mohammad or Jesus

Is God not much greater
Than any name we know
Dressed in different clothes
To be there for all.

KIND WORDS AND KIND THOUGHTS

Kind words and kind thoughts
Haunt me each day
Bring tears to my eyes
And love to my heart

Sweet gestures of love
Arms full of warmth
Dark shadows are gone
And sorrow no more

The touch of your lips
The joy in your step
Loves light in your eyes
Brings life to my soul.

JOY

I breathe your scent, your warmth
Into my heart, my soul
Feel the touch of your lips
Your hands, head, and body
Building smoldering embers

Melding our hearts and minds
Binding our souls as one
Filling our nights and days
With a dash of life's bliss
Together we find such joy

As one we are climbing
Into the sky we dance
Across rainbows we skip
From star to star we waltz
Into the heavens we go.

Marta Moran Bishop

WINTER

Breathtakingly it glistens
Branches are laden with snow
Limbs dressed in glimmering white
Cold winds blow through tree and bough

Snow flies as horses frolic
Across the fields they doth zoom
Prancing in the wonderland
Jumping, rolling in their glee.

A MONTH OF STORMS

A month of storms that never ends
Week in, week out continue on
Forever, the gray days linger
Except for small peeks the sun hides

Once these snowy days were fun
When sun followed, the world was new
Week in, week out onward they go
Every now and then it comes forth

Those sun filled times are gone for now
Through February's winter days
When clouds cover the bright sky
With luck March will be different.

SPRING

Light green, bright green, dark green too
Budding leaves upon the trees
Spring has finally come today
Overnight it seems to me

Yesterday the limbs were bare
Just little nubs upon the trees
Now the buds have opened up
Dressed the trees in green again

Sunlight playing in the leaves
Birds all darting in and out
Building nest to house their young
Singing songs of love and play

On the birth of this new day.

SLEEP NOW

Shush, go to sleep dear tree
The cold winds are coming

Your leaves have all fallen
Their glory is gone

Dark branches stand starkly
Against the gray sky

Soon the snows will lie deep
Lakes and rivers will freeze

Cold winds will blow strong
Upon your bare limbs

All too soon the warm breeze
Will blow from the south

Again buds will pop out
Upon your long limbs

Rest now lovely tree
While the cold winds blow.

Marta Moran Bishop

HONOR

Through the clouds bright sunlight shines
With a golden caress it skips
Through the fields and over the hills
Touching all with loving fingers

All along the river it plays
Melding its laughter with the song
Of the tinkling, cascading brook
They move as one through hill and dale

Sunlight and river dance along
Passing the graveyard where you lie
A prayer is said between the two
In hushed voices they praise your life

Honoring all you were and did
For country, home, family, and love
The fallen hero's one and all
Brook and sun sing in memory.

The two continue on their way
Blessing those still with us today
Who quietly devote their lives
To keeping us all safe and free.

In Memory of those who served and in honor of
those still serving.

About the Author

Marta Moran Bishop lives on a small farm in Massachusetts with her husband, cats, and horses. Ms. Bishop, believes all life is sacred and that everything that is, has emotions and thoughts.

She has been writing since she was six years old, when she wrote, what she describes as the worst play ever written. However, it did not stop her from continuing to hone her craft.

A love of reading and writing fills her life. "I can find something interesting to read even from the back of a box of Oatmeal." She defines herself as emotional, and empathetic.

You can find her on Facebook, Twitter, BestsellerBound, LinkedIn, www.martamoranbishop.com.

You can find her books on amazon.com, barnesandnoble.com, Smashwords, and your local bookstores and specialty shops.

An Authors Note

Sometimes, I feel as if I cannot help myself. The words need to flow, covering pages, notebooks or scraps of paper. Whatever I can find to put pen to paper, jot down and idea, a line that haunts me or a feeling that needs to be expressed.

In Sunlight and Shadows, the verses are based on events that happened and on the way I perceive the world. *Lost Ones,* was written after the shooting at Newtown. I believe it is in how we deal with despair, whether we can learn, grow and find our way back to the light that defines us as human beings.

The light can be found both inside of ourselves and outside in the beauty of the world, the little animals, a friend, or someone we cherish.

The similarity between Sunlight and Shadows and A Poet's Journey: Emotions, are in how they express this roller-coaster we call life.

We as humans all have our emotions in common. Each person may define these feelings of loss, love, anger, and betrayal differently, yet we all suffer them. Some of us have lived with and through things others may not have, but each of us is vital to the knowledge and growth of the human race.

An Authors Note

Nothing and no one in this life should ever be taken for granted or considered to be less vital to the world and all that is in it.

My sincere hope is you will find within these pages a kindred spirit or a new way of looking at

Innocence and Wonder, like Wee Three: A Mother's Love in Verse, is written from the perspective of a child, and is full of verses that range from bugs, dogs, pigs, and nature. It is a terrific book written to charm and enthrall the child in all of us.

Ms. Bishop has once again produced a book to entertain those of all ages and help us see the world as a place of wonder and joyful simplicity.

If you enjoyed Shel Silverstein, you will surely fall in love with Innocence and Wonder.

Wee Three: A Mother's Love in Verse, is a collection of poetry and verse written through the perspective of a child. It was begun in 1924 by Ms. Bishop's grandmother, Helen Springer Moran, and finished by Marta Moran Bishop. It is reminiscent of the days before the computer and television, when imagination was the key to a child's mind.

Wee Three, is guaranteed to make you smile, laugh, and remember the days of your own youth.

It is a highly entertaining read for both children and adults and will delight the reader with its simple verses. If you enjoyed, A.A. Milne or Robert Louis Stevenson's children's verses, you are sure to love Ms. Bishop's, Wee Three: A Mother's Love in Verse.

Dinky: The Nurse Mare's Foal, is the story of one little foals fight for survival after being taken from his mother within hours of his birth. Dinky takes us on a poignant trip through the heart and mind of an animal, who was born for the sole purpose of bringing his mother to milk. Considered by the elite of the horse world, a by-product, 'junk foal.'

Dinky's story will resonate with animal lovers, as well as anyone who has adopted. Although a horse, his story has been called an adoption story. The reader can follow him through the heartbreak, cruelty, loneliness, and finally to happiness in his forever home. His story is based on true events, as each event from the moment the author met Dinky actually happened, though it is the author's interpretation of what he might have been thinking and feeling during the occasions described in his story. His early life which is unknown has been fictionalized by the author and constructed through research and imagination.

There are many wonderful animal rescue leagues, who have empathy toward these small animals, however they are not all sympathic to them. Since, Ms. Bishop has no knowledge of Dinky's early days she used the latter to enhance the strength of his story.

It will break your heart, open your eyes, lift your heart, and teach you much about horses. It is suitable for all ages.

The Between Times:

Marta Moran Bishop takes the reader through a possible future. Unlike Orwell's, Animal Farm and 1984, or Ray Bradbury's Fahrenheit 451, The Between Times is not based on the government 'Big Brother,' but rather it is written using today's ruling by the Supreme Court that corporations are people. In The Between Times, we are shown the possibility of a world where the poor are considered to be a beasts of burden, good only for the labor they can produce or the war they can fight, to enable the war profiteers to make more money.

Poor women are only useful for breeding and considered to be property of men. There is no real way for the poor, who are uneducated to move up in this society, and the middle class is gone.

In this short novel, The United States has taken a social, economic, and cultural step backwards, to a time when our world consisted of lords and serfs. The only thing that keeps those who are not in the ruling class of the elite going is the belief in a prophecy, that one day a girl will be born who will have the ability to unite all kindred spirits past, present, and future, to bring change to the world.

A truly amazingly imaginative book.

A Poet's Journey: Emotions, is Ms. Bishop's first book of adult poetry. In its pages, you will find the good, bad, and beautiful of being human. It is divided into six categories, Love, Death, Betrayal, Nature, Villain or Hero, and Silly Me.

The verses include a glimpse into the heart and soul of one woman, who lived through an emotional roller-coaster year, yet retained her ability to see the silly side to things and beauty in the world around her.

If you like poetry, this is the book for you, if you have grown up thinking poetry is difficult to understand, pick this book up for within it, you might find something that will resonate with you.

A Poet's Journey: Sunlight and Shadows:

Marta Moran Bishop continues her journey in Sunlight and Shadows. This book of poetry, unlike A Poet's Journey: Emotions, is a more thought provoking book. In its pages, Ms. Bishop, deals with everything from God, to life after death, war, and the shooting in Newtown, Connecticut. Still she is able to bring to life the beauty and grandeur of her surroundings and make us laugh, cry, think, and feel.

Sunlight and Shadows will once again take you on an emotional journey through life.

The Void:

The Void, the first true paranormal short story written by Marta Moran Bishop. It will take you deep into the mind and heart of someone either living through a serious mental illness or possibly something mysterious and dangerous resides in the void.

Altori's sister disappeared in the void and Altori barely survived it. Will Altori return to the void again, to search for her sister? If she does will she survive?

The Void is reminiscent of Alfred Hitchcock or the Twilight Zone of later days.

www.ingramcontent.com/pod-product-compliance
Lightning Source LLC
Chambersburg PA
CBHW071735020426
42331CB00008B/2050